The Moment We Met

by Ian Buckley

Published by Playdead Press 2015

© Ian Buckley 2015

Ian Buckley has asserted his rights under the Copyright, Design and Patents Act, 1988, to be identified as the author of this work.

A CIP catalogue record for this book is available from the British Library.

ISBN 978-1-910067-32-1

Caution

All rights whatsoever in this play are strictly reserved and application for performance should be sought through the author before rehearsals begin. No performance may be given unless a license has been obtained.

This book is sold subject to the condition that it shall not by way of trade or otherwise, be lent, resold, hired out, or otherwise circulated without the publisher's prior consent in any form of binding or cover other than that in which it is published and without a similar condition including this condition being imposed on the subsequent purchaser.

Playdead Press
www.playdeadpress.com

The Moment We Met was first produced at The Baron's Court Theatre, London, in March 2015, with the following cast:

Liz Lewis   Mary Drake

Alan Barr   Daniel Lillie

Directed by Ian Buckley

Drama Consultant Harry Landis

Designed by Cleo Harris-Seaton

Lighting and stage management by Phoebe Salter and Leo Bacica

Note from the Playwright

Reading a tv magazine one day, I suddenly became gripped by a story that was both terrifying and moving. It focused on a woman, an amazing ordinary woman, who - having suffered a personal tragedy - was trying to make sense of the aftermath. Central to that process was her utter commitment to finding out the truth about what had happened and who had been involved. Only when she had found answers to these questions would she feel any sense of worth. She needed the truth and she needed justice and this is what drove her on.

This story then is the source and wellspring of THE MOMENT WE MET...

Ian Buckley

Ian Buckley

Ian went to Christ's College Cambridge from the Elliott Comprehensive in Putney and, having obtained an Honours degree in English Literature and a soccer blue, he then gained an MA from The University of Kent, researching the works of Sean O'Casey.

Ian has had a number of plays performed on the London fringe: *Picasso's Artful Occupation* (Baron's Court Theatre); *The Tailors' Last Stand* (Baron's Court Theatre); *Keeping Faith* (The King's Head); *First Timers* (The Duke's Head); *Suits and Blouses* (The Room at The Orange Tree); *Down The River* (Theatre Royal, Stratford East, touring show); *Tainted Love* (The Young Actors' Theatre).

He's been shortlisted for the following playwriting competitions: the Verity Bargate Award; the Maddermarket Award; The Bruntwood Manchester Royal Exchange (long shortlisted with *The Return*); the Brockley Jack 'Write Now Three' competition.

He's had a play on BBC Radio Four, *Changing Gear*; it was re-broadcast in translation on Hessische Rundfunk in Germany, who also broadcast *The Revolutionary*.

The rumour that he's made any money from his pen is entirely unfounded.

Characters

LIZ LEWIS	*40 - works in school office*
ALAN BARR	*31 - firefighter, local station*
TIME	the present
STYLE	the play weaves monologues with naturalistic scenes

NOTE ON CHRONOLOGY: Liz is 40 and Alan 31 at the point where the play begins. They first met four years prior to this. The main events they recall in their monologues and 'remembered' scenes span a period of 8 years.

Woman, 40

Bare stage

Chair

Liz   ...I knew there was something between us the moment we met.

There were three of them. He was the oldest. Gentle eyes.

I showed them to their pitch. Popped over now and then to see how they were doing. He always had a smile.

They were a hit with the kids. 'Mister can I drive your engine?' 'Can I put a fire out, please mister please.' I noticed lots of our young mums suddenly showed an interest in the fire service.

He was good, even when some of the children got into the cabin and started fiddling with things.

They had to go early. Seemed quiet after that...

Alan   ...John's son went to the school, John's my best mate, I said yes.

She seemed to be organiser-in-chief. She showed us to our place, saw we were alright, came back a lot. Were we ok, were the kids playing up? (*He smiles*) When she spoke she spoke to me.

Kids are a laugh - kept asking me if I'd start a fire so they could put it out. Little sods were into everything. Even the cabin. If we'd stayed any longer they'd've had our axes away.

Later I couldn't find my key - the one opens all the tender compartments. Either someone'd nabbed it or I'd dropped it. I'd give the school a ring...

*Out of **Alan**'s monologue, into scene as remembered by **Alan***

*Phone rings. **Liz** picks up phone*

Liz   Hazeltree School.

Alan   Hi...I was there...the fireman.

Liz   Sam's Dad?

Alan   He's John. I'm the mature one.

Liz   Hope you've recovered. Our kids can be little devils when they get excited.

Alan   Yeah...kept us on our toes.

Liz   Thought you were patient.

Alan   Was I? Were we?

Liz   'Specially you.

Alan   Have to don't you. Could be the firefighters of tomorrow.

Liz   You're getting a thank-you letter from all the juniors.

Alan   I'll frame it.

Liz   Were you phoning for anything special?

Alan   God yeah...I've lost my key. Wondered if anyone'd handed it in...

Liz   Not so far as I know.

Alan   I love that key.

Liz   Tell you what, why don't I take a look? I know where you were.

Alan   I don't want to be any trouble.

Liz   I'll ring you back.

Alan   It's T-shaped.

*Out of scene, into **Liz**'s monologue*

Liz   ...I must've got lucky because it was the first thing I saw. The grass was flat with all the tramping. Good thing I got there before the kids, bunch of magpies.

        I rang him back - he'd pick it up later. Don't ask me why but I started to watch the clock. Liz, I said, get on with your work, there's enough of it. By the time it got to four I had a knot in my stomach. At a quarter past I thought, not coming, time to go...

*Out of **Liz**'s monologue, into scene as remembered by **Liz***

***Alan** enters office as she's preparing to leave*

Alan Sorry I'm late. Fires never seem to fit in with my shifts.

Liz Is this it? *(Shows him key)*

Alan Oh you diamond. It is. You've saved my life.

Liz Hanging offence is it?

Alan Firing squad at dawn.

*Out of scene, into **Liz**'s monologue*

Liz ...As I heard his voice I got a feeling. The one I had when I first saw him. Like warm water washing over me.

It wasn't till Janet the cleaner barged in that we left. We said bye outside my house. I thought you won't see him again.

*Out of **Liz**'s monologue into **Alan**'s monologue*

Alan Funny how you bump into people once you know them. Couple of weeks after the school thing, I'm driving back from a call-out when who do I see, lugging two big bags, but her. I give her a big hallo. Her face lights up. I say, joking...

*Out of **Alan**'s monologue into scene as remembered by **Alan***

Alan Give you a lift?

Liz I'm nearly home.

Alan	I'm still over the moon about my key. If there's anything I can do…
Liz	Two weeks in the Caribbean wouldn't come amiss.
Alan	I'm down that travel agent's right away.
Liz	*(Laughing)* Or you could take me for a drink. 'S cheaper.
Alan	*(As lights change)* Whoops, lights. What's your number?
Liz	*(Loud)* 355673…

*Out of scene as remembered by **Alan**, into **Alan**'s monologue*

Alan I had no trouble hearing. Tell you the truth I was a bit… Women don't… she must like me I thought, to give me… She seemed nice. I'd give her a bell…

*Out of **Alan**'s monologue, into **Liz**'s monologue*

Liz …The next night he phoned. I hate it when the phone goes late… I panic. *(She stops, tearful)* When I heard it was him I relaxed. He was sorry it was so late, he'd been out on a call and had just got back.

We agreed to meet in Caffè Nero. I love it. People chatting away in languages I don't understand. Makes me think I'm abroad when I'm just round the corner.

I had a skinny latte, he had a cappucino. Once we got talking there was no stopping us. We seemed to have so much in common. This man - chats about everything, makes me laugh - he's great.

We started to meet on a regular basis - same place, same seats if we could, by the window. We never ran out of things to talk about. It was like we struck a match and it burst into flame. In the end I decided to ask him back to mine...

Out of Liz's monologue into Alan's

Alan   ...So after a few months of meeting in Café Whatsit, Liz invites me back to hers. I want to say no but it's a friendly invite, I don't eat so well I can turn down the chance of a good meal and anyway I'm beginning to like her...

What I'm saying is I was happy with things as they were - once a week, a good chat and a laugh. If it sounds hard to believe because it's a man talking about a woman sorry it's the truth - women and me didn't seem to mix. If it'd been up to me we'd've stayed as we were. Liz was the one who pushed it.

Out of Alan's monologue into Liz's

Liz   Looking back I should've gone with my brain not my heart. Then we'd've stuck at friends. He pushed it. He wanted more. I could see it in his eyes. I could feel it - the way he looked at me, brushed against me sometimes.

I won't deny I had feelings for him. He was a ray of sunshine. I knew if I saw him, no matter how bad my week'd been, he'd make me laugh. And isn't it one of our fantasies - to be rescued from the flames by some gorgeous fireman who's also kind, gentle and fabulous in bed?

*Out of **Liz**'s monologue, into scene as remembered by **Liz***

***Alan** sits in comfy chair. **Liz** sits on sofa near him*

They sip wine

Alan   Nice place.

Liz   Thanks.

Alan   It's got soul.

Liz   What's yours like?

Alan   Basic.

Liz   If that suits you...

Alan   A question of convenience.

***Liz** stands, goes to hi-fi, puts on CD – tuneful, romantic MOR rock-pop*

Liz   Dance. I won't bite.

*She pulls **Alan** to his feet, puts her arms round him. They dance*

Liz   Not shy are you Alan? Never thought of you as shy.

Alan   Neither did I.

*They dance – a smoochy. **Alan** begins to relax*

Liz Ages since I've danced. You?

Alan A hundred years.

Liz You're that old?

Alan Had my letter from the queen.

Liz ...You can hold me tighter. I won't break.

Alan holds her tighter

They dance more and more slowly till they stop

They look at each other

Slowly they kiss

Lights down

Lights up

Alan and Liz sit on sofa

Alan That was wow. *(Liz says nothing)* Was it...?

Liz ...Wow for me?

Alan Yes.

Liz Yes.

Alan But you didn't...?

Liz No.

Alan Because of me.

Liz Yes, it's all your fault.

Alan It is.

Liz ...Or it could be mine. I'm so irresistible...?

Alan D'you think I'm rubbish?

Liz I think don't make such a thing of it.

Alan *(He puts his hands on his pelvis)* You can work on these. To improve...

Liz Better get working then.

Alan *(Decides)* Did you like the bits we were doing before...?

Liz I like to get on with it.

Alan Right. Me too.

*Fade out of scene and into **Liz**'s monologue*

Liz That was the first time. If I said it was a mountain-moving, earth-shattering, hold-on-to-your-seatbelts, lights exploding in my head moment I'd be lying. He was gentle. He tried to give me pleasure as well as take it.

*Out of **Liz**'s monologue into **Alan**'s monologue*

Alan When she tore my clothes off I thought god she's passionate, will I measure up? But the more we did it, the more she cooled off till in the end I thought she's giving me pleasure but is she getting any herself?

*Out of scene as remembered by **Alan**, into **Liz**'s monologue*

Liz After he went I had a think. It's your first time in years, what d'you expect? Passion needs practice. Yes we know you were spontaneous when you were young, yes, we know you went wild at the drop of a hat but things happen... people change. Tonight was a step in the right direction.

*Out of **Liz**'s monologue, into **Alan**'s monologue*

Alan The way it happened that time was how it happened all the times after. Liz'd start like she was on fire but fade. I could feel the moment. She'd work hard to get it back but it was from here... *(Taps head)* ...not here. *(Taps stomach)*

There were things about Liz that didn't make sense. Was the 'up-for-a-laugh' Liz a front? An attractive woman who liked company but lived on her own? Who'd clam up in the middle of a sentence like she'd gone off with the fairies... who wanted to make love but didn't seem to enjoy it when it happened...

*Out of **Alan**'s monologue, into **Liz**'s*

Liz He never did anything he wasn't sure I was fine with. It was a question of mutual respect. On that basis, bit by bit, I built my trust. We'd spend the odd night together. It was nice having someone round the house, 'specially when you knew they'd be leaving in the morning.

I invited Mum and Dad round to meet him. I made them promise not to bring things up I didn't want him to hear. I had nervy tummy all evening in case they did but they were as good as gold. They liked him.

Maybe because he'd met mine I wondered more and more about his. Who were they? What they were like. Why didn't he talk about them?

*Out of **Liz**'s monologue, into scene as remembered by **Liz***

Liz I've been thinking...

Alan Sounds bad.

Liz ...You never talk about your family. Why not?

Alan Dunno.

Liz What are your Mum and Dad like? You do have a mum and dad?

Alan Never beat me more than once a day - let me out of the broom-cupboard twice on Sunday.

Liz Spoiled rotten then.

Alan They were good to me.

Liz Where do they live?

Alan Pretty near.

Liz See much of them?

Alan No.

Liz   Don't you get on?

Alan   Yes. They're the greatest.

Liz   God I'd love to meet them. I bet they're interesting. Are they interesting?

Alan   Very.

Liz   Can I meet them? You don't want me to do you?

Alan   ...I do.

Liz   I can feel it.

Alan   How about next Saturday?

Liz   Saturday's fine. I'm excited already. Sorry if I pried.

Alan   No you should.

Liz   Goody, I'll pry some more. You absolutely and totally sure you don't have a wife?

Alan   I told you, no.

Liz   You've never had one?

Alan   Never. You sure you don't have a husband?

Liz   None I remember.

Alan   And no kids?

Liz   *(With an effort)* No.

Alan   End of questions.

*Out of scene as remembered by **Liz** and into **Alan**'s monologue*

Alan Law of life - get to know people, they'll get to know you. If you want to be private, live in a rain-forest. I never liked people knowing my business but Liz wasn't people, she meant a lot to me, more every time I saw her. She had a right.

*Out of **Alan**'s monologue and into scene as remembered by **Alan***

***Alan** and **Liz** scramble up a grassy incline. They puff*

Liz *(As they do)* What a lovely area. Are they rich?

Alan Sort of.

Liz It's amazing.

***Alan** stops walking. They're high up. He looks ahead. To the right, to the left*

Alan Stop.

Liz Here?

Alan Just here.

Liz Where are they?

***Alan** and **Liz** sit*

Alan Look't that. Takes your breath away.

Liz Are we meeting them here?

Alan Yep.

Liz   Not at their house?

Alan   No.

Liz   Will they be long?

Alan   ...They're here already.

Liz looks round

Alan   You're sitting on them.

Liz   What?

Liz stands up sharply. Looks at ground where she's been sitting

Alan stays sitting

Alan   I scattered Dad's ashes here. *(He shows **Liz** where he did it)* Mum's on top of Dad's. They loved this place. It was their favourite.

Silence

Liz   This isn't funny.

Alan   I'm not laughing.

Liz walks away

*Out of scene as remembered by **Alan** and into **Liz**'s monologue*

Liz   ...I didn't know whether to put my arm round him, or tell him he had a funny way of doing introductions.

Why hadn't he just told me they were dead? If he thought what he'd done was normal he'd got a funny idea of normal.

Slow down, Liz. Your parents are alive. You don't know how you'd act if they weren't. Maybe this is his way.

Later, when I looked back, I wondered if that was the moment my feelings for Alan changed. On that hill, with that view, where he'd scattered his Mum and Dad.

*Out of **Liz**'s monologue into **Alan**'s monologue*

Alan It was my way of doing it. I took a chance. She might never've spoken to me again. For a while I thought she wasn't going to. But I could see she was moved which was all I wanted. For once I'd maybe done something right.

*Out of **Alan**'s monologue into **Liz**'s monologue*

Liz The drive home was quiet. I hate silences but I couldn't say a word. He drove me to my door, I just about said bye.

We didn't speak for weeks. In the end I rang to ask him round. I got a few things in - cold chicken, potato wedges. Wine.

It was a nice evening. I had the feeling back, the being washed in warm water one. His voice made me feel good. He looked fit.

*Out of **Liz**'s monologue, into scene as remembered by **Liz***

***Liz** and **Alan** sit at table. They've eaten. **Liz** drinks wine, **Alan** beer*

Liz   Sorry about that day on the hill.

Alan   Sssh.

Liz   I should've said something.

Alan   No you shouldn't.

Liz   ...How did they die?

Alan   Accident.

Liz   What sort?

Alan   Car.

Liz   ...Were you with them?

Alan   I was at home. The phone rang. 'Is that Alan Barr?' 'Yes.' 'Are your parents Ronald Barr and Elizabeth Barr?' 'Yes.' 'Of 141 Parkview Road?' 'Who is this?' 'The police. We'd like to talk to you.'

They drove me to a hospital. They slid Mum out. She didn't look at peace. *(**Alan** stops)* Then Dad. Their heads weren't the right shape and they'd shrunk. Jesus, I thought, you two need a jump-start. Where's my leads? Clip them to your toes and switch on the current.

	I could touch them but they weren't going to touch me. Ever.
Liz	How horrible.
Alan	It wasn't Dad's fault. He swerved to miss a car coming at them. On their side of the road.
	She was on her mobile - the other driver. So busy chatting she hadn't noticed. She blamed Dad. He was on her side. She didn't know how she'd missed him. She hadn't been on her mobile - that was a lie.
	They nailed her. They're not thick, the police. Tyre marks. Mobile phone records. People think they can lie but they can't.
	She changed her story after that. If that's what the police said she'd have to believe them. Yes she had answered her mobile. Her mother was ill, that's why. She was sorry but it wasn't on purpose.
	A year's ban. What she got. For killing Mum and Dad.

*Out of scene as remembered by **Liz** and into **Liz**'s monologue*

Liz	He was shaking like he was going to shake to bits. He had starey eyes, his cheek twitched then it went - back to the Alan I knew.
	I asked him to stay. We made love. I thought I was dreaming. I'd given up on ever reaching the point I reached that night. My body hadn't shut down.

With the right man I could escape my voice. We danced round the room like kids for hours.

*Out of **Liz**'s monologue into **Alan**'s monologue*

Alan   ...This time it was good. Liz didn't slip away. We climaxed together. It was the greatest feeling. Maybe taking her to see Mum and Dad had broken a barrier. She was warmer. She wanted me.

I stayed more often after that. One day she made me an offer I couldn't refuse...

*Out of **Alan**'s monologue, into scene as remembered by **Alan***

***Liz**'s bedroom*

***Alan** and **Liz** change the bedlinen*

They try and put the duvet into its cover

They get into a mess

Liz   This side up.

Alan   This one?

Liz   No this one...

Alan   Why didn't you say?

Liz   I did.

Alan   Aren't they the same?

Liz   Twist it a bit more why don't you.

Alan   I'm doing my best.

Liz   Not good enough.

Alan   I'll give you good enough

They get tangled up in duvet and duvet cover, end up in heap on bed, **Alan** *tickling* **Liz**

Liz   You're as mad as me.

Alan   And that's saying something.

Liz   Well matched then.

Alan   Couple of nutters.

Liz   Why we get on so well.

Alan   If you say so.

They kiss - passionate

Relax lying on bed

Liz   You can move in if you like.

Alan   Here you mean?

Liz   No the pub round the corner.

Alan   Just checking...

Liz   You'll have to obey the rules, keep clean, stay out of trouble...

Alan   I thought you liked your freedom.

Liz   I'll have to make sacrifices.

Alan I'll have to think.

Liz Not too long - I might change my mind.

Alan I've thought. Yes. Cos you need me.

Liz I need you?

Alan A lot.

Liz I'd say it's the other way round.

Alan We need each other.

Liz Time will tell.

*Out of scene as remembered by **Alan** into **Liz**'s monologue*

Liz He'd been dropping hints about moving in for months. I'd change the subject or say we'll talk about it later. Then one day he caught me off guard...

*Out of **Liz**'s monologue into scene as remembered by **Liz***

***Alan** and **Liz** change the bed*

They try and put the duvet into its cover

They fasten poppers on duvet cover with duvet now inside

Liz First to the middle...

Alan Go.

They fasten them fast, reach the middle at the same time, but...

Liz You got one wrong.

Alan 'S not on my side.

Liz 'S not on mine.

Alan We'll see.

They trace poppers in from each side

*The mistake is in **Liz**'s half*

Alan Told you so.

***Liz** and **Alan** shake up duvet in its cover*

They end up under it giggling

***Liz** pulls herself half out but **Alan**'s completely submerged*

Alan Know what I think? I think I should move in.

Liz Why?

Alan You need me.

Liz Like a dose of the flu.

Alan To help you make the bed.

Liz A perfectly done up duvet is so important.

Alan Also cos otherwise I'll be on the streets.

Liz Meaning?

Alan The landlord wants me out.

Liz Trashed his property have you?

Alan He's selling up.

Liz   By when?

Alan   End of the month.

Liz   That's two weeks.

Alan   Thirteen days to be exact.

Liz   Have you been looking for a new place?

Alan   I can find somewhere if I don't mind sharing with mice and dirt. Now if I moved in here...

Liz   No.

Alan   Till I found somewhere.

Liz   Uh huh.

Alan   Buy you flowers every day.

Liz   No.

Alan   Pay the rent you ask.

Liz   Nope.

Alan   Wash-up, hoover, go shopping...

Liz   Not enough.

Alan   I'll kiss your feet. I'll be your butler and slave.

*Out of scene as remembered by **Liz** and into **Liz**'s monologue*

Liz   ...I didn't give my answer that day. Or the next.

'It's a bigger step for you than him. There are things in your life you don't want to share. Live with someone, that gets more difficult.'

Don't be silly - those things are locked away, in cabinets, you've got the keys. He'll never find them and even if he does he can't open them. I'll get any future letters sent to Mum and Dad's.

When he moved in he was a dream. Kitchen spotless. Beds changed. Shopping done. He was so perfect. Can't you do something I don't like? Lick your plate, fart in public, have BO.

But it was fine. He made me happy. True the feeling came and went but before Alan it hadn't even come.

Our life was good. If anything began to build up he gave way. That suited me. I like to be boss.

Out of Liz's monologue, into Alan's monologue

Alan I loved her. I wouldn't cross her. I was her lodger. I paid my rent. She had the say. She was one step above me in the chain of command, like at work, with the commissioner and men.

Out of Alan's monologue into Liz's monologue

Liz ...I respected him and he respected me. We chatted a lot, we laughed, we did things together - that's how we were.

After a few months I noticed we were talking about babies a lot. He was always bringing the subject up. Weren't they cute? Would he make a good dad? I'd make a good Mum.

Liz, I said, lighten up. It's a normal subject. Maybe he wants to be a Dad.

I made myself talk about them. Once or twice I even made a joke about having one. *(She stops, distressed)*

Out of Liz's monologue, into scene as remembered by Liz

Scene in living room. Sofa

Liz enters, glass in one hand, bottle in other

Liz slumps onto sofa, a bit drunk

Some wine spills onto her dress

She giggles, wipes it off

Liz   Alan? Where are you?

Slumps back, dreamy

She feels her hair tugged gently from behind

Liz   Whassat? (She giggles)

Again she feels her hair being tugged

Liz   Owh.

*Suddenly **Alan** springs up from behind sofa. Falls forward over sofa back, ending half upside down next to **Liz***

Alan   *(Still upside down)* You look good.

Liz   Why are you upside down?

Alan   You turn me on.

Liz   Or am I upside down?

***Alan** lets himself slip onto sofa. Twists himself upright*

Alan   I want to… you know.

Liz   Bit decadent, isn't it? Middle of the day.

Alan   Go where it takes you.

***Alan** starts to kiss Liz. She responds. Passion takes over. They move to the essential*

Liz   You've forgotten…

Alan   Can't we do it without?

Liz   I'm not too old y'know. To have a baby…

Alan   Long as I'm with you. With a child. Without one. You're the light. The lamp.

Liz   You want to take a chance?

Alan   I'm a gambler.

Liz   You want a baby…?

Alan   With you.

Liz Long as some other poor... whatsit looks after it.

Alan I'm ready for a full-on dad experience

Liz Mad.

Alan ...Change nappies, make food, walkies...

Liz Up in the night yes...when it cries?

Alan Babies are like fires - once they kick in you shift your butt.

Liz And of course, you'll give up your whatever... to look after the whatsit.

Alan If it's right.

Liz Words. They're... something...

Alan Cheap?

Liz Thassit...cheap...

Alan Pure gold. Like my heart.

Liz *(Sign with fingers and thumb indicating lots of chat)* You'll do this, you'll do that. You're all talk.

Alan You're the one's talking. I'm ready for action.

Liz Ooh. Well...action...

Alan You'n'me making love. How action is that.

Liz *(Sarky)* Oh please give me a baby...I mean thrill... *(She laughs)*

Fade down on them making love

*Out of scene as remembered by **Liz**, into **Liz**'s monologue*

Liz   ...He got me drunk, laid on the charm. *(Reflects. Switch)* That won't do. You can't blame him. You knew what was what. He made the running but you fell into line.

Admit it come on - maybe you wanted a child. Your biological clock was ticking. Alan was good to be with...

*Out of **Liz**'s monologue, into **Alan**'s monologue*

Alan   ...I noticed Liz loved to talk kids. Her sister had three. A friend had twins. Once, when she was telling me about a friend who was pregnant, I said, 'Is that what you'd like - a baby?' I wish I hadn't. The way she looked at me... I thought she was going to cry.

One day after a boozy lunch she surprised me...

*Out of **Alan**'s monologue, into scene as remembered by **Alan***

***Alan** and **Liz** sit on sofa*

*He drinks beer from a can. **Liz** has her legs over his lap. She drinks wine*

Liz   Mmm...dreamy.

Alan   ...Mellow.

Liz   ...In the mood.

Alan For...?

Liz What d'you think?

Alan Think? Me?

Liz You in the mood?

Alan Have to try me'n see.

Liz kisses him

They build up to making love

Liz Show me what you can do you fireman you.

He hesitates

Alan ...Hadn't I better...?

Liz Seize the moment.

Alan Isn't it a bit risky?

Liz Am I the love of your life?

Alan Is the earth round?

Liz If I did get pregnant wouldn't you promise to be an ever-loving dad?

Alan That's what I'd be.

Liz Then get on with it.

*Out of scene as remembered by **Alan**, into **Alan**'s monologue*

Alan If anyone wanted a kid it was Liz. Not that the thought of having one upset me. When I thought about it I quite liked the idea.

From then on we made love as nature intended. I deduced that meant she wanted to get pregnant.

When one day - a few months later - she told me she was I said: 'Fantastic. Result. It's what we've been waiting to hear.' We opened a bottle of champagne. Liz drank half a glass, I drank the rest.

*Out of **Alan**'s monologue, into **Liz**'s monologue*

Liz I was amazed how fast I got pregnant. Yes he'd wanted it more than me but I wasn't upset when it happened. I took it as a sign Alan and I were made for each other.

My voice didn't like it. It wouldn't let up, not for a moment, even though I promised it nothing would change.

I still hadn't told Alan. About that. He'd told me things that were sad for him but I hadn't done the same. What was stopping me. 'You have to, you just have to Liz. You're giving birth soon. He has the right to know. It's now or never.'

I chose a Friday. I made a risotto, opened wine, lit candles...

Half past eight - no Alan. Nine, the same. By ten I was worried. Was he alright? Had he had an accident? Say he'd been hurt? I'd just picked up the phone when a text arrived. 'On my way now. Had a problem.'

*Out of **Liz**'s monologue, into scene as remembered by **Liz***

***Liz** paces around living room*

Front door opens off

*Enter **Alan**, limping – bruises round eyes and on cheeks. Talks as if can't open mouth*

Alan   Hi babe.

Liz   Alan - what's happened?

Alan   Nothing.

Liz   You poor thing you.

***Alan** sits down painfully*

Liz   Your mouth…'s all bruised. And your eye. It's nearly closed.

Alan   Hazards of the job.

Liz   A fire?

Alan   You got it.

Liz   What happened?

Alan   A roof collapsed. We were under it.

Liz   So dangerous.

***Liz** hugs **Alan** hard. He hugs her back*

Alan   *(In pain as she hugs)* Not so hard please.

Liz   *(Releasing her hug)* Sorry. D'you hurt all over?

Alan   Every place.

Liz   Your team? Are they...?

Alan   All fine. How lucky were we. The roof collapsed inwards. Down or towards us I'd look like crispy bacon.

Liz   Don't. You're well anyway? Nothing broken?

Alan   I'm fine.

Liz   I'm so glad. I'm just...

***Liz** hugs him hard, shaking with relief and emotion*

*Fade down on scene as remembered by **Liz**, into **Liz**'s monologue*

Liz   ...Seeing Alan like that knocked any thought of telling him things clean out of my head. After that there never seemed a right moment. Something always got in the way.

*Out of **Liz**'s monologue into **Alan**'s monologue*

Alan   ...We decorated a room for baby. One day I was putting bags of stuff in the loft when I notice two filing cabinets at the back, almost like they'd been hidden. I should'n't have cos they weren't mine but I gave them a tug, see if they'd give...

*Out of **Alan**'s monologue, into scene as remembered by **Alan***

Kitchen. Meal eaten

***Alan** washes up*

***Liz** sits at table*

Alan   I put the stuff we bagged in the loft.

Liz   Oh.

Liz looks away, says nothing

Alan   Some filing cabinet thingy missed my toe by that. *(Makes sign with finger and thumb)*

Liz   They didn't come open?

Alan   They're locked.

Liz   How d'you know?

Alan   How do I...?

Liz   ...They're locked? Did you try and open them?

Alan   ...No.

Liz   Yes you did.

Alan   I did not. Alright I gave a little try, to make sure they wouldn't spill.

Liz   I knew you had.

Alan What's in them anyway?

Liz Things.

Alan I know that.

Liz ...Letters and stuff from school. Hey Babyworld rang. We can pick the cot up at the week-end.

Alan Excellent.

Liz Thought you'd be pleased.

Alan How is baby?

Liz Busy. Have a feel. Come on.

Alan kneels, puts head on Liz's stomach

Alan It moved.

Liz Letting you know.

Alan Boy or a girl?

Liz One or the other.

Alan You don't say.

Liz Can't wait now.

Alan Me neither.

Liz Get baby-room finished, that's it.

Alan Two more days it'll be done.

*Out of scene as remembered by **Alan**, into **Liz**'s monologue*

Liz ...Shortly after I gave birth to a 7 pound beautiful baby girl. A little miracle. When they put her on my chest I was in heaven.

We called her Dawn. She was a new start.

Out of Liz's monologue, into Alan's monologue

Alan She was cracking, she was the best. I loved her from the moment I saw her.

My life was back on track. I'd put it there. You ever thought how your life can turn on a nothing - something you wouldn't think at the time was important? If I'd said no to the Hazeltree day - and I nearly did because I had other things planned - I wouldn't've met Liz, we wouldn't've had Dawn, all the great things that happened to me, wouldn't have happened.

'This is a dream,' I'd say. 'It's got to be. My life can't be this good.' But it was. It was through and through totally amazingly brilliant.

Out of Alan's monologue, into Liz's monologue

Liz ...I took maternity leave. I needed to bond with Dawn. Alan worked.

We had lots of visitors. Mum and Dad. Alan's firemen mates. Life settled into a routine with Dawn at the centre. I concentrated on her.

I told myself things would have to be put on hold. That's how it would have to be. Not to worry, it wasn't for long.

*Out of **Liz**'s monologue into **Alan**'s monologue*

Alan Life was sweet. I was the man who had everything. The more days passed, the more I believed it would last. I planned our future. Two more children, bigger house, promotion. As long as it was with Liz life'd be fine.

Sometimes I thought how great it would've been for Mum and Dad to have known Liz and Dawn...

*Out of **Alan**'s monologue into **Liz**'s monologue*

Liz ...About two months after the birth I found out something that rocked me.

I'd taken Dawn for a walk - the only way to get her to sleep sometimes - and I'd bought the local paper. I got home and sat down for a read. I turn over a page and there it is. 'Local Fireman Guilty Of Assault.' I read it again and again. Then I just sat. For ages.

*Out of **Liz**'s monologue into scene as remembered by **Liz***

*Kitchen, **Liz**'s house*

***Alan** and **Liz** in kitchen*

Liz What's this...?

*Liz hands **Alan** the paper opened at the important page*

***Alan** reads*

***Alan** walks out of the house*

Liz   Alan? Where are you going? Alan - come back.

*Out of scene as remembered by **Liz** and into **Alan**'s monologue*

Alan   ...I couldn't believe it. I'd got through the whole thing without her knowing and now when I thought it was behind me... 'For Christ sake Alan,' I said, 'Get back in there and tell Liz the truth.'

*Out of **Alan**'s monologue and into scene as remembered by **Alan***

*Kitchen, **Liz**'s house. As before*

Liz   ...You didn't get those bruises fighting a fire, you got them fighting a man.

Alan   It wasn't just me. All the lads were.

Liz   I can't believe you could lie to me like that.

Alan   I'm sorry.

Liz   Why?

Alan   I was scared...

Liz   Of what?

Alan   Just...was...

Liz   *(Warmer now)* Because you got into a fight?

Alan Yes.

Liz Have a bit of confidence in me. *(Liz moves close to Alan. She puts her hand in his)* Promise you'll tell me the truth in future.

Alan I promise.

Liz Silly man.

Alan Wonderful woman.

Liz You've got a fine to pay.

Alan Yep.

Liz And bound over to keep the peace.

Alan Not a problem.

Liz How did you get into a fight in the first place?

Alan We go for a drink, someone hears we're firefighters, they come and ask us - for no good reason you or I or anyone else can think of - who the fuck we think we are and to come outside and they'll show us. You can't back down. It's your pride. You can't let them get away with that.

Liz If it was the other man's fault, how come you were found guilty?

Alan The police never get it right.

Liz Why not?

Alan When they arrived I was winning. The copper sees that and thinks - he's on top, he must've started it. The other guy's hardly going to tell him he's wrong.

Liz What am I going to do with you?

Alan I could tell you.

Liz You walk away if someone insults you.

Alan I'll try.

Liz And drink in a nicer pub.

Alan We do now.

*Out of scene as remembered by **Alan**, into **Liz**'s monologue*

Liz ...He'd hidden everything from me except his injuries. Since they were impossible to hide, he'd invented a story about them...

*Out of **Liz**'s monologue, into **Alan**'s monologue*

Alan ...It'd come out - that was a relief... I'd hated hiding it. Since when was getting into a fight the worst thing in the world? Covering up like I did was a lot worse than a few fists flying.

I was getting so wound up about losing Liz I was starting to do silly things, things I wouldn't normally do, things that were out of character cos normally I'm honest.

> I hadn't told her what the guy'd said that'd made me lose it. That the only reason I was a fireman was so I could make it with the women I saved.

*Out of **Alan**'s monologue, into **Liz**'s monologue*

Liz   ...I asked Alan how he'd stopped letters coming to the house. 'I had them sent to the station.' And meeting solicitors and going to court? 'I'd tell you I was working.'

It was about then he started to have bad nights. Had I made him feel bad about what he'd done? But I hardly mentioned it and when I did we'd usually end up having a laugh. I was sure I hadn't made too much of it.

*Out of **Liz**'s monologue, into scene as remembered by **Liz***

*Bedroom **Liz**'s house. Double bed. Three in the morning. Sidelight on*

***Alan** tosses and turns. Sits up in bed. Gets up, creeps out of room. Creeps back*

***Liz** wakes*

Liz   Alan?

***Alan** gets back into bed, sits up staring ahead*

Liz   You alright?

Alan   Fine.

***Liz** tries to sleep*

Alan fidgets. After a bit he creeps out of bedroom

Liz listens

Alan re-enters. Liz sits up

Liz Can't you sleep?

Alan I checked on Dawn.

Liz She okay?

Alan Fast asleep.

Liz lies down, awake now

Liz Want a drink?

Alan Go to sleep.

Liz You sure?

Alan I'll read.

Liz Night.

Alan Night... *(Liz falls asleep)*

Alan sits staring

Out of scene as remembered by ***Liz****, into* ***Alan****'s monologue*

Alan ...It'd been a blip. It didn't change a thing. Liz and I got on better than you could've thought. Dawn got lovelier. Any time I wasn't working I took her for walks, changed her nappy, rocked her to sleep. I loved it. Being a dad. Great days. Great great days.

*Out of **Alan**'s monologue and into **Liz**'s monologue*

Liz …One ordinary kind of evening Alan was late. No probs - a fireman's life. I got on with things but then it got to the sort of late-time I start to worry.

In the end I phoned his work. 'D'you know where Alan is?' 'Sorry… we don't.' 'You've no idea?' 'We're not sure if he's on a call or he's knocked off. Can we ring you back?' I phoned John. He didn't know either. I had a feeling people weren't telling me things…

END OF PART ONE

INTERVAL

PART TWO

Liz's monologue continues from last scene

Liz ...I had a feeling people weren't telling me things. I rang his mobile. I texted. What was going on?

Out of Liz's monologue, into Alan's monologue

Alan ...Then something happened that changed my life. It was like a mine exploding under me. Blew everything in pieces up into the air.

Out of the blue, I get a call on the station internal. Will I come to the office, someone wants to see me. I walk down, there's a guy I've never seen before with the gaffer. He's police he says, they need to talk to me. What about? He'll tell me when we get to the station.

There are two more coppers waiting outside. I know them both from the fires we've been on. One's called Danny - we've shared a few drinks. We drive to the station and they take me to a room. We sit down and the one I don't know warns me anything I say may be taken down and all that stuff.

This is what he says. The DNA matching whatsit place - whatever it's damn well called - has told them my sample matches a person who's wanted for a crime. 'What d'you mean 'my DNA'? How d'you know it's mine?' 'We know it's yours because we took it from you.' Then I realise when - after the fight, the swab-in-the-mouth don't-gargle-please job. 'So what's the crime this supposed-to-be my DNA's linked to,' I say...

*Out of **Alan**'s monologue, into **Liz**'s monologue*

Liz ...The phone rang. My heart thumped, this had to be Alan, it just had to be.

*Out of **Liz**'s monologue, into scene as remembered by **Liz***

Both on phone

Alan Hi love.

Liz Alan. Are you alright? I've been worried sick.

Alan I'm fine. There's been a mix-up.

Liz Where are you?

Alan ...Police-station, Heppel Road.

Liz Is it on fire?

Alan Can you come down?

Liz Aren't you coming home? What's going on?

Alan I'll explain when you get here. Can you come?

Liz I'll have to bring Dawn.

Alan You can't.

Liz What will I do with her?

Alan Ask your parents to have her.

*Out of scene as remembered by **Liz**, into **Liz**'s monologue*

Liz   ...I left Dawn with Mum and Dad and drove to the station. They searched me. Alan was only getting this visit because they knew him. It was against the rules.

They took me down to a corridor full of cells, unlocked a door, Alan looked pleased to see me.

*Out of **Liz**'s monologue, into **Alan**'s monologue*

Alan   ...They gave me a few more details. *(Reflects)* They did that alright.

I said, 'It's surreal. I can't help you on this. I haven't got the faintest idea what it's about. I'm a fireman. I put my life on the line for people like you every day of the week, to see you and your dearest don't burn to death. Can I go? Danny, tell him. I've got a partner. We've got a baby.' 'Sorry mate.' 'You're joking?' 'We're definitely not joking.'

'Can I see Liz then?' 'Not allowed.' 'I won't try anything. I promise. On my baby's life. Just five minutes.' The one I didn't know looked at Danny. 'Five minutes. As you're a friend of Danny's. We trust your promise.'

*Out of **Alan**'s monologue into scene as remembered by **Alan***

Cell in local police station

***Alan** sits in cell*

Liz enters

Cell door is left wide open

Alan *hugs* ***Liz***

Alan Am I pleased to see you.

Liz I'm pleased to see you Alan. I thought you might've been in hospital or something...

Alan Not this time.

Liz Why are you here?

Alan *puts finger over his mouth to indicate she should speak quietly. From now on they do*

Alan You think I know?

Liz ...Are you saying you don't?

Alan It's some mad mix-up like happens to me about once a month.

Liz Mix-up about what?

Alan I don't know. Can we forget about it for two minutes? What've you been up to?

Liz Coming here. Being searched. Told they're taking a chance letting me see you. What's going on?

Alan ...Some nonsense about blood samples...

Liz ...Blood samples?

Alan I can't say anything till I know more...

Liz ...You can tell me what they told you.

Alan How can I...?

Liz About the blood samples.

Alan They've mixed mine up with someone else's.

Liz They said that.

Alan I say that.

Liz What does it matter if they have?

Alan What it matters is - according to them - that this other person - the one they've got me mixed up with - has done something wrong.

Liz Like what?

Alan I don't know.

Liz Didn't they tell you?

Alan No.

Liz They can't keep you here without telling you what you've done.

Alan Why would I want to know? 'S nothing to do with me.

Liz Yes but... Alan you do know something...

Alan Can we change the subject?

Liz Tell me what it is or I'll go and ask. *(Loud now, losing it)* I mean it. *(Pause)* Right.

Liz strides to cell door

Alan   Rape.

Silence

Liz   Sorry?

Alan   I heard that word. That's what they said.

Liz   Rape?

Alan   Keep your voice down.

Liz   *(Quiet)* He raped?

Alan   Yes. *(Spelling it out)* R. A. P. E. Aren't I speaking English?

Liz   When did he?

Alan   I don't know.

Liz   A month ago? A year?

Alan   I don't know. Ages.

Liz   Just tell me how long ago for god's sake!

Alan   Six years I think? Yeah I heard six.

Liz can hardly keep herself together

Alan   Liz? Liz? Are you alright?

*Out of scene as remembered by **Alan**, into **Liz**'s monologue*

Liz ...I must've fainted or something because next thing I know I'm in a strange room staring at Mum and Dad. Mum's holding Dawn who's giggling and gooing.

I put her to my breast but my milk wouldn't come. A woman they told me later was a doctor suddenly loomed up. 'D'you feel well enough to go home? You look much better dear. You fainted. Follow it up with your GP.'

Mum and Dad stayed for a time. 'I feel fine now,' I said. 'Back to normal. You don't need to worry.' 'If you're sure.' My amazing Mum and Dad. What would I do without them?

I'd put the phone on answer and turned off my mobile. Alan left message after message. He'd been remanded in prison - would I visit?

Jean my solicitor rang. She had important news, could we meet up?

I don't know how many weeks slipped by. In the end I filled in the visitors' pass.

Out of Liz's monologue, into Alan's monologue

Alan ...I was remanded to Wandsworth. 'Ask to be put on rule 45. You'll live longer,' Andy said. So I did.

I had the right to sixty minutes of visits a week. Liz saved them up. She wanted all of me in one go. She was missing me as much as I was missing her.

They gave me a lawyer. Young bloke, confident. Said they couldn't convict me on DNA alone. Would I tell him everything I remembered about nine years ago even if it was hazy.

...It's a pattern, I thought, how my life goes. I build something good - bad luck wrecks it...

I was innocent. Liz had to believe me. I hadn't raped anyone. I knew nothing about it.

*Out of **Alan**'s monologue, into **Liz**'s monologue*

Liz   ...I'd wanted to tell Alan about me for so long but somehow I never got round to it. Something got in the way. Well this was it, this time...

I took Dawn to Mum and Dad's and drove to the prison.

*Out of **Liz**'s monologue, into scene as remembered by **Liz***

*Note: everything that happens between **Alan** and **Liz** does so in a prison visiting area*

There are other prisoners with visitors though at a distance. There are prison officers. We hear all this but don't see it

*We see only the table where **Liz** and **Alan** meet*

***Liz** sits at empty table*

***Alan** arrives at table. **Alan** gives **Liz** hug, sits facing her, holding her hand*

She gives him bar of chocolate which he eats

Alan   How are you?

Liz   Fine... all over the place...

Alan   Me too. Like I'm in some fantasy world.

Liz   Waiting to get back to reality.

Alan   I've got a lawyer.

Liz   Is he good?

Alan   If the way he talks is anything to go by he's a genius.

Liz   He can get you off?

Alan   The case against me's going nowhere. How's Dawn?

Liz   With Mum. I couldn't...

*He offers chocolate to **Liz**. She refuses*

Liz   Alan... I... want to tell you something. About me.

Alan   Yeah?

Liz   I should've told you before. I've wanted to for ages...

Alan   Okay.

***Alan** puts his arms round **Liz**. A warm quiet moment*

Liz   It's just... I'm getting a cold and I'm worried Dawn'll catch it.

Alan   Um?

Liz   Sneezing, runny eyes…

Alan   That's not it.

Liz   It is. I'm worried about Dawn.

Alan   …It was bigger than that.

Liz   Her health is very big.

Alan   Look, if you don't want to say… even though I'm wondering… like I have been for months.

Liz   Wondering what?

Alan   About you.

Liz   You don't need to wonder about me.

Alan   Fainting? In the police station? You've never come near to fainting before.

Liz   I told you I hadn't eaten for…

Alan   …The cabinets in the loft? Padlocks you need an acetylene burner to cut through. For school-books? No one padlocks books.

Liz   I do.

***Alan** gets hold of her arm across the table. Strong grip*

Alan   Just tell me what you were going to tell me. Is it to do with your Mum and Dad?

Liz   I told you…

Alan   …Did your Dad try something on you?

Liz My Dad's an angel. Don't you dare say a word against him!

Alan Is it to do with when you were young? Something happened? You had a... an abortion... a miscarriage...?

Liz Shut up.

Alan Am I getting warm?

Liz Let go of my arm.

Alan Be honest with me.

Liz You're hurting me.

Alan I told you about my parents. I was honest with you.

Liz It's nothing to do with honesty.

Alan Whatever it's to do with, be it. *(Nothing from Liz)* Because you love me then. You love me and you want to tell me.

Liz I've told you.

Alan If you don't say, I won't tell you a single other thing. Not one more thing.

Liz Don't be silly.

Alan D'you know how irritating that is? You go to tell me something then stop.

Liz I was worried my cold would...

Alan You don't respect me, that's what it comes down to. If you did you'd tell me. I thought we had something better.

Alan lets go of Liz. She feels her arms tenderly

Alan ...I'm going back to my cell.

Alan turns his head, half rises. He's about to call a prison officer when...

Liz No don't. I'll tell.

Alan sits

Liz You asked me once if I had kids. I said no. It was a lie.

Alan A lie?

Liz Let me say what I have to say. I had a child. A girl. I wasn't much more than a child myself. When the father, who was as immature as me, disappeared it was Mum, Dad and me who brought her up. It worked. I had a life. I saw my friends, I partied. Later, when I was earning, I found a flat near to my parents. My daughter and me were like that, like sisters. We were so close it was... I'd've died a hundred times to save her...

Alan What d'you mean save? From what?

Liz ...From harm is what.

Alan Like any mum.

Liz I wasn't there for her. When she needed me. I didn't even say goodbye.

Alan What d'you mean didn't say goodbye? What are you talking about? Why didn't you?

Liz Because she was dead that's why. And daughters don't come back from that, not even to say goodbye to their mothers.

Alan Dead? Jesus wept...

Liz D'you want to know how she died?

Alan Well if you...

Liz With a knife. After she was raped. Raped and then stabbed. That's what she went through before she left us. And I didn't even know. My daughter was being... was being... and I was at home thinking she was enjoying herself...

Alan Christ almighty...

Liz *(Half crying)* So now you know...

Alan That's...

Liz grabs Alan

Liz That's it. Except I want to find the man who did it. That's the thing that's kept me going. Knowing one day I'll find him, come face to face with him...

She digs her nails into his arms. Stops

Liz releases her grip. She's drawn blood

Liz   Only now it's harder. I've got you and Dawn. *(Switch)* The other man - the one they've mixed you up with - he's only accused of rape isn't he?

Alan   Yes.

Liz   Thank god for that.

Out of scene as remembered by Liz, into Alan's monologue

Alan   ...Neither of us felt like chatting after that. After a bit Liz said she had to go. She'd visit in a month. 'With Dawn?' I said. 'If I can.'

...I sat there. I looked at my arms. *(He sucks the blood from the wounds)* Tried to take it in.

Out of Alan's monologue, into Liz's monologue

Liz   ...I picked Dawn up from Mum and Dad's and went home. I fed her and put her down. A letter had come. I knew who from. 'Open it Liz, go on.' I was shaking so much I couldn't read. 'Deep breaths, come on, deep breaths...'

'Dear Liz, I'm unable to reach you by phone so I'm writing. There have been dramatic developments in your daughter's case. Please contact at once. Jean.'

I picked up the phone, dialled, stopped, stood up, sat down, put Dawn in her pram and went for a walk. I walked till my legs ached. I came back, picked up the phone, dialled, stopped.

Just then it rang. 'Mum, am I glad to hear…' 'Hi Liz. Jean here. Can you come to the office?' 'N…not now. Dawn's asleep.' 'As soon as she's awake get a cab and come over will you? I'll pay.'

I sat in Jean's office. She couldn't stop smiling. 'They've found a match. For Amy's killer. After all these years? They've got him Liz!' 'How did they get a match?' 'He was in a fight. Town-centre. They took a sample.'

'Do they ever get them wrong?' 'What wrong?' 'The samples?' 'Mix them up you mean? Hardly ever.'

'What's his name - the man?' 'Barr. Alan Barr. He's a fireman.'

I felt I'd been hit with a hammer. I could've collapsed with no return. So many thoughts rushed through my head. Alan? My Alan? I had to hang on or I'd go mad.

I got the name of the DNA place from Jean. I found it on the web. I read every entry that had to do with mistakes and muddles…

Samples had been mixed. Mistakes had been made. It was there, on the screen. And more than one. Thank god, I said. Alan had nothing to do with it. It was a mistake.

*Out of **Liz**'s monologue, into **Alan**'s monologue*

Alan   ...I didn't know at first the girl who'd been raped and murdered was Liz's daughter. The reason I didn't was, though the girls' first names were the same, their surnames weren't. Liz's is Lewis, the dead girl's was Grant. When Liz told me her daughter used her father's name and that was Grant... *(He trails off into thought)* That was tough - the toughest since Mum and Dad died...

*Out of **Alan**'s monologue into **Liz**'s*

Liz   ...The visits were weird. I'd sit there looking at him, wondering... then forcing myself not to.

*Out of **Liz**'s monologue into **Alan**'s*

Alan   It was awesome. Liz was with me. She had faith in me. She kept pushing me, questioning me...

*Out of **Alan**'s monologue into scene as remembered by **Alan***

Prison visits room

***Liz** and **Alan** seated as before*

Liz   ...Jean says they've checked and double checked. There's no mistake.

Alan   What d'you expect? They're not going to admit it are they.

Liz   When Jean told me that, I started to think, how could your... your... get on Amy without you knowing?

Alan It's not worth thinking about...

Liz D'you want to prove you're innocent?

Alan Of course I do.

Liz Then it is, it is worth it! I've got a theory. Someone planted it.

Alan My sperm?

Liz It's the only way.

Alan A pervert who wants to murder a young woman'll do anything. You worked out how?

Liz You were having sex with a girl. One of the ones you told me about, that used to hang round the station. The murderer was watching. He saw where you put your used durex - in a bin or something. He waited till you went then he took it. Now he could murder any girl and you'd get the blame.

Alan That's... what a diabolical bastard. To think of something like that

Liz Is that what you did?

Alan *(Startled by question)* Is what what I did?

Liz Used a Durex when you slept with girls?

Alan Yes I did. For their sake as well as mine. I always took precautions.

Liz ...There's one thing that doesn't fit.

Alan What?

Liz They've only found your sperm. If my theory's right, there'd be yours and his.

Alan You're right. How then? How could that work...? *(Thinks)*

Mm... yes... yes... say this man only murdered Amy? I mean say he didn't have sex with her, say that wasn't his thing. Then he used my sperm to confuse the police?

Liz It's possible I suppose.

Alan More than. Be perfect for a bastard like that. *(As if it's just come to him)* Hold on...thought of another way. Don't go mad at me alright... I'm just supposing...

Liz Say it please.

Alan Just... well just say I had sex with Amy...

Liz Uhhhh.

Claps her hands over her ears

Alan I'm just supposing. Hear me out.

Liz takes her hands away

Liz Quickly then.

Alan Say Amy and me had sex then later that day someone - another person - murdered her.

Liz Why would they?

Alan A boyfriend say?

Liz She didn't have one.

Alan A boy who thought he was her boyfriend then?

Liz She had friends who were boys - she didn't have a boyfriend.

Alan All you need is one of these friends who're boys to *think* he's her boyfriend - that's all you need. He finds out she's slept with someone, he'd feel betrayed.

Liz You said you never met Amy.

Alan There were so many girls hanging round Liz... I don't remember every name.

Liz You could have sex with my daughter and not remember her name?

Alan I'm not saying I did. I'm saying if...

Liz Amy didn't sleep around.

Alan She probably didn't but who would know? What does any parent know about their kid? What did my mum and dad know about me? How I was with my mates? Not a lot and thank god cos I don't think they'd've approved of some of it.

*Out of scene as remembered by **Liz** into **Alan**'s monologue*

Alan Liz believed me. I saw the doubt go from her eyes. That made me feel good. My life was worth Jack shit if I didn't have Liz. I had the feeling I was winning...

*Out of **Alan**'s monologue into **Liz**'s monologue*

Liz I wanted to believe him, I really did but something was nagging away - making me question, making me doubt, making me worry...

I went back to Jean. I told her the two theories - one Alan's, one mine - as if I'd thought of them both. 'That'll be their defence. An unknown man taking Barr's used sperm to smear on Amy's body after he's murdered her. Or Amy just happening to be murdered by an unknown man on the same day Barr's had sex with her.' 'Couldn't it happen?' 'Just about.' 'Just about means it could.' 'You seem to want this man to be not guilty, Liz?' 'I want him to be guilty but it has to be sure.' 'It's one hundred and ten per cent sure.'

'I want to drop the charges.' 'You want to what? You can't. It's not up to you, it's up to the CPS. *(Change)* ...Liz, it's a lot to take in. You can't believe it but it's true. You're finally going to get justice for Amy. What you've fought for for all these years.'

I picked Dawn up from Mum and Dad's and took her home. I lay down with her till she went off. I must've gone off too because I could hear my voice calling out to Amy and that only happens when I'm dozing.

'Amy? Speak to me. I miss you. I can't wait to join you... but... I've got Dawn now, we have to look after her. And I have to find him. Help me. Tell me who killed you darling. Was it Alan? It wasn't was it? Tell me it wasn't darling girl.'

She didn't. Since Alan'd moved in she'd hardly spoken. She thought I was neglecting her but I wasn't. I never would. As long as I lived I'd never neglect my beautiful girl.

I went into a dream I hate. A man was on top of Amy, in a clearing in a wood, raping her. I could never see his face, it was always turned away. As he raped her she cried out for me. He didn't stop. He reached his climax and got off.

She lay there choking and crying. I'll never forget her eyes. Never as long as I live. The look in them. He took a knife, a shiny knife with a black handle, stood over her and stuck it in.

I woke up. I was shaking, my skin was wet. There was Dawn, a few inches from my face, sleeping like an angel.

As I lay there I heard Amy's voice. So faint. What was she saying? Was she telling me something? 'Mum, I'm here.' 'Where?' 'Where I've always been. Near to you.'

'Oh Amy, sweetheart, love of my life, I can hear you.' A wave of joy went through me. 'Don't leave me like that again, you hear. I don't like it.' 'No Mum, I won't. I'll be with you from now. You and Dawn. When you've got rid of him.' 'Who?' 'The man who murdered me.' 'Alan?' 'I've got to leave you Mum. I'll be back when he's gone.'

I lay awake for ages. Dreams aren't real, I said, they're not truth, they're worries coming out. You can't rely on dreams.

I got up, made myself tea. If I just thought about nothing then the truth would come to me. Just work and think about nothing that's all I wanted to do.

*Out of **Liz**'s monologue into **Alan**'s monologue*

Alan   I hadn't seen Liz for over a month. I had to know how she felt. She was my lifeline. I'd go under without her.

...I kept telling myself, you didn't do it. You went off the rails when Mum and Dad died, you hated the girl who killed them, you fantasised about how you'd make her pay. You even scared yourself - what you'd to to her when you found her. But you didn't find her. And Amy wasn't her so why would you hurt Amy?

*Out of **Alan**'s monologue into **Liz**'s monologue*

Liz   …Alan left a message. 'I'm going mad for not seeing you. Don't do this to me. I've sent you a pass. Visit me. I love you.'

Then I remembered - how could I have forgotten? In two weeks it would be the biggest day of my year. I'd visit. On that day if I could. I sent in my visitor's pass.

*Out of **Liz**'s monologue, into scene as remembered by **Liz***

Same prison

Background noise of prison visits room

***Liz** waits, seated at table, expectant*

***Alan** enters room escorted by a warder (unseen)*

*He sits at table facing **Liz**. Own clothes*

Alan   Hi love.

Liz   Hi.

***Alan** takes **Liz**'s hand. Holds it in his*

Alan   You look fantastic.

Liz   Thanks.

Alan   I love your hair. And your top. Black and red.

Liz   My hair's not red.

Alan   Golden.

Liz   Auburn.

Alan   I love it whatever it is.

Liz   How are you?

Alan   Great - time of my life.

Liz   I've put your clean clothes in reception.

Alan   Thanks. How's Dawn?

Liz   Well.

Alan   Couldn't bring her?

Liz   I don't want to break her routine.

Alan   ...Not even for her Dad?

Liz   I'll bring her next time.

Alan   Bet she doesn't even know I've gone.

Liz   She looks round as if she misses someone.

Alan   Me?

Liz   Who else?

Alan   She misses her Dad, she misses me.

Liz takes two muffins from chair, puts them on table

Liz   They wouldn't let me bake a cake. This was the best I could do. *(Liz hands Alan a muffin)*

Alan   They look good.

Alan takes cellophane off muffin

Liz　　It's Amy's birthday today. She'd've been twenty-seven.

Liz takes chain with pendant on it from her neck

*She opens pendant and shows **Alan** photo*

Liz　　That's her. On her seventeenth.

Alan　*(Looks)* She's pretty.

Liz　　Such a lovely day. Family in the afternoon, friends and family evening. Everybody danced. Amy loved dancing - hear a beat, have to move. Just like her Mum. Shall we sing Happy Birthday to her?

Liz sings quietly

Liz　　"Happy birthday to you / Happy birthday to you..."

Alan　*(Joins in last bit)* "...to you..."

Liz　　*(Together)*

Alan　*(Together)* "Happy birthday dear Amy / Happy birthday to you."

Liz　　Three cheers. Hip, hip...

Alan　...H'ray.

Liz　　Hip hip...

Alan　H'ray

Liz　　Hip hip...

Alan   H'ray.

Alan takes bite of muffin

Liz   If you'd killed Amy you'd say wouldn't you?

Alan   Liz...

Liz   You'd tell me wouldn't you?

Alan   I didn't.

Liz   ...The police keep saying...

Alan   The police keep saying, they keep saying. They've got me so wound up with their saying they're making me confused.

Liz   About what?

Alan   Things?

Liz   Be a big thing to block if...

Alan   I said I was confused. I didn't say I'd blocked anything.

Liz   You might've though? Blocked it?

Alan   They say people block the big things.

Liz   Is that what you've done?

Alan   Not unless I'm different to the person I know. Have you seen me different?

Liz   Since when? I've only known you since the school fete.

Alan And Caffe Whatsit. I loved that place.

Liz I didn't know you before.

Alan ...Chatted about everything, didn't we? Remember we tried to guess what people did for a living from how they looked?

Liz Amy used to meet there. Saturdays. Before it was Caffè Nero. By that window.

Alan tries to hug her. She pulls back

Alan You and Dawn are the only people matter to me. The rest of the world could die tomorrow...

Liz If Dawn died you'd know how it feels.

*Out of scene as remembered by **Liz**, into **Liz**'s monologue*

Liz ...I sat in court every day. I heard in detail about Amy's last moments. I felt connected to her which was my only joy in the horror of how she died.

The main evidence was the DNA. The fact it had been found in and on Amy. That it belonged to Alan. Or there was a one in billion chance it didn't.

The fact he hadn't reported for work the night Amy died. *(She thinks about this)* As he said, flu is flu - it has to run its course. He hadn't mentioned it though.

They made a lot of his character... his obsession with bedding women. The bet he'd made to be the first of his team to score a hundred. His arrogance. The way he domineered.

His defence was what Jean'd said - mismatch and cross-contamination and an unknown man. They asked me questions about our life together. I spoke about the Alan I knew.

The trial took three days. The jury took four hours. 'Have you reached your verdict?' 'Yes.' 'Guilty or not guilty?' 'Guilty.' 'Is it unanimous?' 'Yes.' The judge sentenced Alan to life with a tariff of twenty years.

*Out of **Liz**'s monologue, into **Alan**'s monologue*

Alan ...As the judge read the sentence, Liz looked at me. She had tears in her eyes. I read her lips. 'They can't do this to you.'

*Out of **Alan**'s monologue and into **Liz**'s monologue*

Liz ...I looked right through Alan as the judge read his sentence. I couldn't bear to look him in the eye. I didn't know what I might be looking at.

I went home. Dawn was in a lovely mood. I fed her. I cleaned and tidied. My mind was blank.

Next day I went back to work. I got into my routine. Mum agreed to have Dawn while I found a child-minder.

A few weeks later I visited. I drove to Reading. I felt like I had lead in my veins. I sat in a room away from the main visiting place. A door opened. Alan came in. He was wearing a striped blue shirt and blue trousers.

My stomach fluttered but it wasn't the nice flutter I had when I first met him. He sat down. A guard stood just near.

*Out of **Liz**'s monologue, into scene as remembered by **Liz***

Single visiting room, off main visiting room, prison

Bare walls, table, two chairs

***Alan** sits opposite **Liz**. He wears prison-issue clothes*

He looks drawn

He takes her hands in both of his

She takes them away

Alan   God I've missed you...

Liz   You murdered Amy. After you raped her. The last thing she knew in this life was not a hug from me or a laugh with a friend but a knife into her body from you.

Alan   Jesus wept...

Liz   One thing you can do, one pathetic thing, is admit it. It won't make up for it in any way but you can do it.

Alan What's happened Liz?

Liz I've thought and thought till I can't think any more. You did it.

Alan You turn against me I'm dead.

Liz Admit what you did. For the things we've shared. For Dawn.

Alan says nothing

Murderer. You're a murderer. I hope your conscience tortures you till the day you die. If there's a life after death I hope you rot in it for evermore. I never want to see or hear from you again. In twenty years when they let you out, Dawn and me will've long gone. From today we're dead to you, like Amy's dead to me. *(Liz pushes back chair)* ...Unless you admit what you did.

Alan ...If you want me to.

Liz I want you to tell the truth. (She stands to go)

Alan For Christ sake don't go.

Liz Did you rape and murder Amy?

Alan ...Yes.

Liz Say it.

Alan I raped and murdered Amy.

*Liz sits back down. Looks **Alan** in the eye*

Liz Why?

Alan I don't know.

Liz You can't do a thing like that and not know.

Alan I'm twisted. I'm an animal. I'm from hell.

Liz They're not reasons.

Alan I can't think of a reason.

Liz Because your character changed after your parents died? Could it have been that? Because of how they died? Like was said in court?

Alan Yes.

Liz That was a terrible shock, it changed you, you lost control.

Alan I was out of control after that crash.

Liz You weren't normal. You were on the edge. You murdered Amy but you saw the girl who killed your parents?

Alan It must've been that.

Liz Tell me what happened. From the moment you saw Amy, till you left her dead.

Alan Jesus Liz.

Liz Start now.

Alan You know what happened. It was said in court.

Liz I want to hear it from you.

Alan For Christ sake why?

Liz You can tell it from the inside.

Alan I can't remember...

Liz I'll help you shall I? November eleventh, nine o'clock, you saw Amy.

Alan Liz...

Liz Where did you see her? Where, I said.

Alan ...Laysdon Road.

Liz Where in Laysdon Road?

Alan At the lights .

Liz She was in her car on her mobile?

Alan Like they said.

Liz When you saw her doing that you got angry? It brought back memories?

Alan I wanted to talk to her. Before she caused an accident.

Liz So you followed her?

Alan Yes.

Liz Out of town till she parked on the Denholme Road near the Elrose Estate...

Alan If you know this why are we going over it?

Liz She parked her car and got out. It was dark. She should've kept to the pavement where she could be seen but she didn't. She took the path through the little wood. It was quicker. What did you do?

Alan I parked near her and got out. I wanted to tell her she could... well kill someone. Chatting like that. I followed her.

Liz To tell her?

Alan Yes.

Liz No. You knew from the moment she went that way, you were going to rape her...

Alan I wanted to tell her about her driving.

Liz How do you talk to someone in a wood in the dark?

Alan It wasn't that dark.

Liz Why didn't you tell her then leave?

Alan Because when I got into that place ...something took me over. Yes, that's right it... turned me into someone else. It made me do things I don't do.

Liz It made Amy undress did it?

Alan It did everything.

Liz It raped her did it?

Alan Yes.

Liz   Why didn't it let her live when it'd finished raping her?

Alan   I don't know.

Liz   Shall I tell you? Because your 'something' didn't fancy the idea of going to prison.

Alan   It has to be...

Liz   And that's why you, not it, stabbed Amy. Because you wanted to make sure she wouldn't live to testify against you. It was her life against a few years behind bars for you and she lost. *(Alan says nothing)* Nice while it lasted was it? Did you get off on it? The sex? The power? Over her body? Over her life? The kick as you killed her? As you stuck the blade in? D'you remember it now and then and get the thrill back?

But it's not your fault is it. It's the 'something' that took you over. That's who we have to blame.

She stands to go again

Alan   Please Liz. I'm begging. I didn't mean to do it. It wasn't me.

Liz   I'll go through this with you. We'll look at everything - when you were a baby, growing up... everything. If for a fraction of a second I think you're lying to me, it's finished.

Alan   I'd never do that.

Liz   That's what we'll do. That's what you and me will do. Work to understand how you could do something as horrible as that.

Out of scene as remembered by Liz, into Liz's monologue

Liz   I hate him. Last time I went there he held my hand. I pulled it away. I can't have any contact.

He's Dawn's father - she has a right to a father - but he raped and murdered Amy. He deserves to die.

Sometimes when I think I had a child by... I can't eat for days. I want to give my insides a scrub out.

When I look at Dawn I have to not think who her father is. I have to shut it out. It's not her fault, it's nothing to do with her. She's not to blame.

Each visit I ask more questions. Each time he gives me a new detail I get closer. To being sure... to the time I can say yes, *yes* he did it. He's the one. No room for doubt. When I get there, and I nearly am, I'll kill him.

I've started to work out how. It won't be easy but I'll find a way, that I know. When I'm sure, I'll kill him. For Amy's sake.

Out of Liz's monologue into Alan's monologue

Alan   ...I call it a miracle. We're still in love. After everything that's happened the feeling's still there.

When I hold her hand, when I squeeze it, I know. The way she looks at me...

I've told Liz what I did and how I did it. It's the only thing she wants to hear. She drinks it in, she wants to know more so she can understand. Sometimes I spin it out a bit... for her.

I'm trying to make up for something you can't make up for. I'm sure I did it... the shrink says I've blocked it and I'm going with that because well, she's qualified, she should know.

I'm trying to work out why... that's what the therapy's for - to find out why, what made me do it.

It was possibly this. I was in a bad place. On the edge because of what'd happened to Mum and Dad. The hate against the other driver built up till it took me over. And because of that I ended the life of a lovely girl who hadn't done anything to me, who didn't even know me.

That's what it could've been. I still can't remember it all... what happened. I hit a wall. The shrink says I'll climb over it in the end...

I worship Amy, I worship her memory. I know her through Liz. The more I know her the more I love her. She was a fantastic young girl. She was the centre of Liz's life. When she lost Amy it broke her heart.

I'll be fifty one when I get out. Liz will be sixty, Dawn will be twenty one. I know Liz'll stick by me. That's the power of love. Overcomes everything.

I'm lucky. I've found a saint. That's what Liz is - a saint. She'll save me. That's what saints do.

LIGHTS FADE

THE END